When The Well Runs Totally & Completely Dry

IDEAS AND ACTIVITIES FOR GRADES 1-6

Created By
Becky Freeman

Broadman & Holman grants the buyer permission
to reproduce the activity pages contained within for classroom use only.
Any other use requires written permission from Broadman & Holman.

© 1996 Broadman & Holman Publishers

What do you do with those "in-between" times?

You know those times when:
- a child shows up earlier than you expected.
- your lesson went a little faster than planned and there are still five minutes left till departure time.
- you want to re-inforce a lesson and are just fresh out of ideas.
- you are providing child care during adult meetings such as choir, special Bible studies, committee meetings, etc.
- you are thirsting for fresh ideas but the old well of ideas is dry as a bone!

What's a teacher to do?

Your long drink of water is here. This book is overflowing with activities to quench your thirst for ideas. The pages are perforated for easy tear-out and duplicating. And the activities are designed to reinforce spiritual truths and teachings for your particular age group.

So, go ahead. Take a sip, then settle back and gulp down the soothing flow of refreshing ideas.

Ahhhhh!

That's The Truth!

God told Jeremiah to look for someone who told the truth (Jeremiah 5:1-2). It is so important to God that we be honest. Color the hearts by the sentences that are true, red. Color the hearts by the sentences that are false, black.

1. Martha was Jesus' mother.

2. Jesus loves everyone.

3. It is okay to lie so you won't get in trouble.

4. Jesus was never a little boy.

5. The children loved Jesus and He loved them.

6. If you are really good at baseball, God loves you more.

7. _____
(You make up one and ask the class to say "true" or "false.")

Jeremiah's Cheer-Up Letter

Jeremiah wrote a letter to cheer up his friends that were being held like prisoners in enemy land (Jeremiah 29). He told them to go on with their lives and try to be happy because God would take care of them.

Do you know someone who could use cheering up? A sick friend or a lonely person or a far-away relative? Write them a cheerful note, draw a picture, then cut out your letter, fold it and tape it. It will make its own envelope and be ready to give or mail.

CHEER-UP LETTER!

Dear _____,

Love, _____

A Happy Drawing for You!

Garden's Surprise

Jeremiah's letter (Jeremiah 29) told his friends to plant gardens and eat the produce. He did not want them to give up living and building and growing good things to eat. Add the numbers and color the picture sections to find something that grows in a garden.

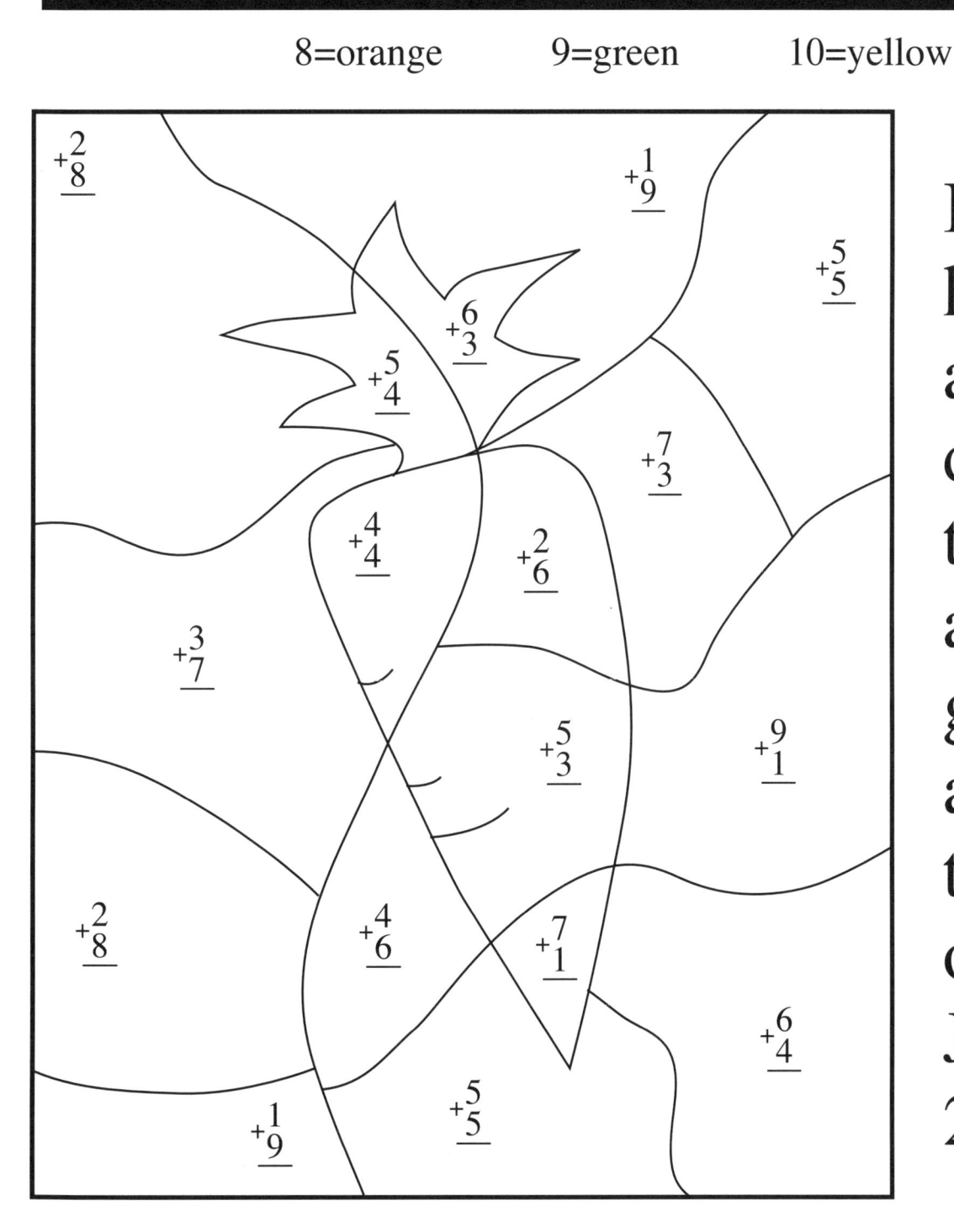

8=orange   9=green   10=yellow

Build ye houses, and dwell in them; and plant gardens, and eat the fruit of them. Jeremiah 29:5

A Tale of Two Builders

Jesus tells the story of two builders (Luke 6:46-49). One builds a house the lazy way, the other one builds his house on solid rock. If we do what Jesus tells us to do, we will be like the wise man whose house stood firm even in time of trouble.

Connect the dots. Draw rain and flood waters. Then, under the pictures, finish the word that tells what the houses were built on.

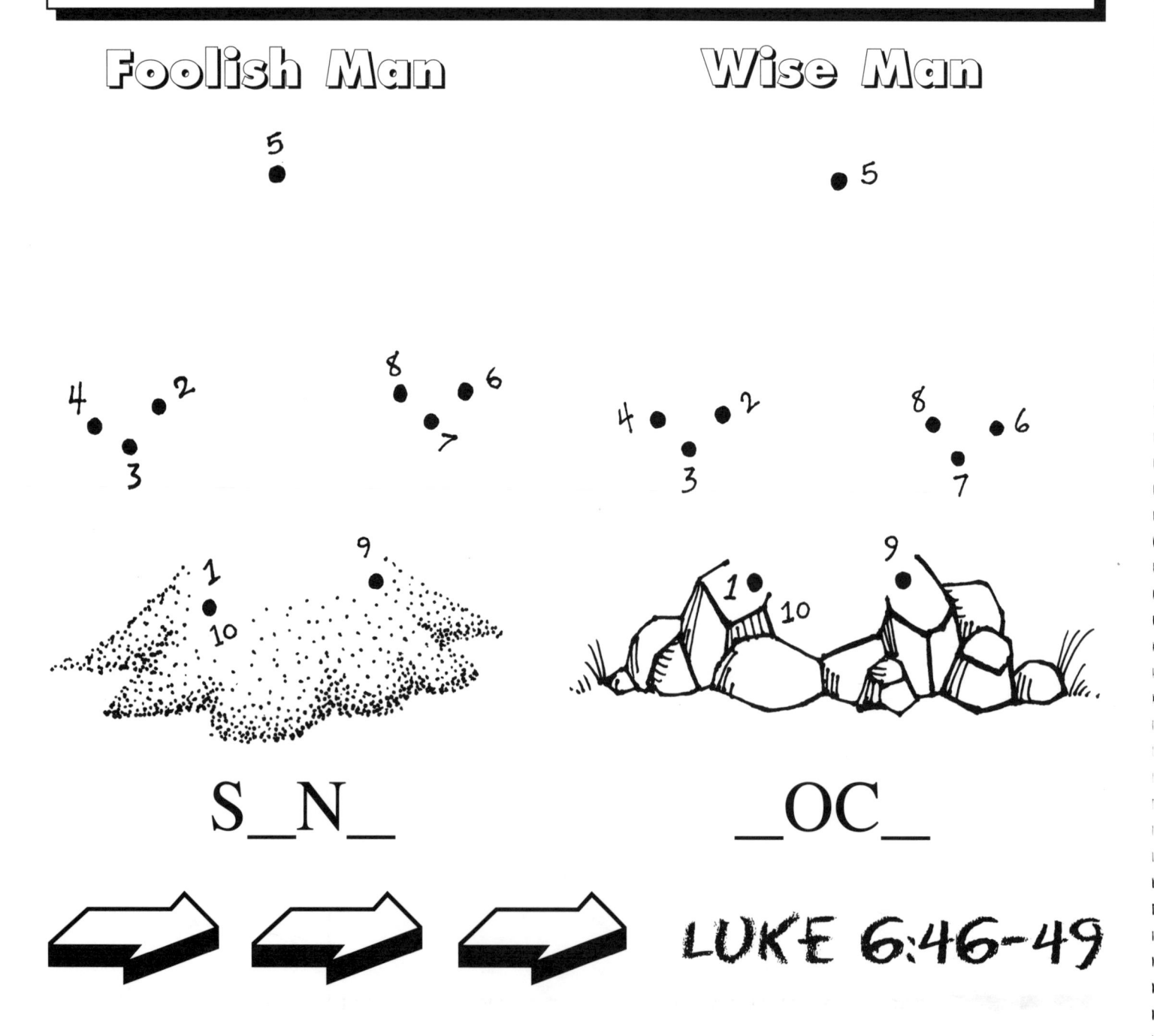

Foolish Man   Wise Man

S_N_   _OC_

LUKE 6:46-49

Try Your Hand at a Thanksgiving Turkey!

Trace your hand below. Then add features to it with a crayon or pencil to make it look like a turkey. On each feather, write one thing for which you are thankful. (Use a dark marker, pen, or black crayon.) Write your name on the turkey's body, where the palm of your hand was. Lightly color each turkey feather with a different bright color.

Example:

The Bible says God writes our names on the palms of His hands! (Isaiah 49:16) We are SO SPECIAL to Him! Doesn't that make you thankful?

Grades 1 & 2. ©1996 Broadman & Holman, When the Well Runs (Totally and Completely) Dry: Ideas and Activities for Grades 1-6

Mystery Treasures

Moses sent spies into a beautiful land called Canaan. They brought something WONDERFUL back for "show and tell." Color the numbered sections according to the instructions to find out what it was. Then read the verses and fill in the blanks with the correct letters and answers.

What did the spies bring back from Canaan? g__p__, p_m_g__n_te_, _i_s
(See Numbers 13:23-24)

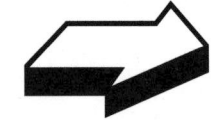

1=red   5=black
2=green   6=yellow
3=purple   7=blue
4=brown

1. Did Caleb say to go get the land or not to go? _____
   Numbers 13:30

2. Why wasn't Caleb afraid? _____
   Numbers 14:9

Optional Teacher's Note: Many children have never tasted a pomegranete or fig. If you can find these at your local grocer, you might bring one for the kids to sample.

6   Grades 1 & 2. ©1996 Broadman & Holman, When the Well Runs (Totally and Completely) Dry: Ideas and Activities for Grades 1-6

A Son's Journey Home

Jesus tells the story of a son who leaves home, only to spend all his money and find himself so hungry he eats with the pigs. Suddenly, one day he decides to go home. He doesn't know if his father will be happy to see him or not. But the father is SO happy to see his son that he gives him a ring and a robe and prepares a celebration feast.

Follow the son's journey through the maze, stopping to draw pictures here and there as instructed.

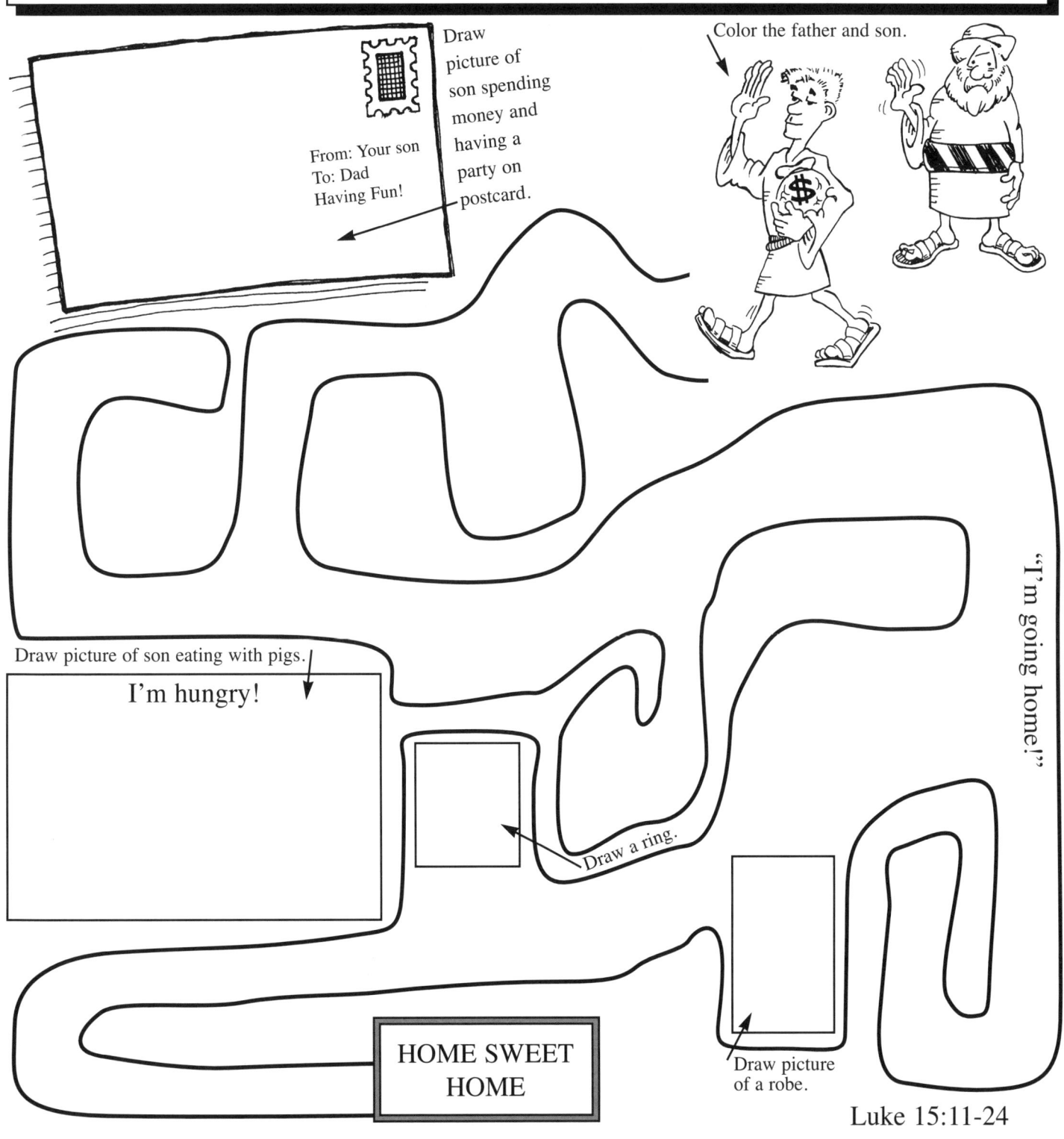

Draw picture of son spending money and having a party on postcard.

From: Your son
To: Dad
Having Fun!

Color the father and son.

Draw picture of son eating with pigs.

I'm hungry!

"I'm going home!"

Draw a ring.

Draw picture of a robe.

HOME SWEET HOME

Luke 15:11-24

Grades 1 & 2. ©1996 Broadman & Holman, When the Well Runs (Totally and Completely) Dry: Ideas and Activities for Grades 1-6

Joyful Flying Angel

Read Luke 2:9-10. The angels brought happy news to the shepherds. Fill in the words on the angel, then cut her out. Put a paper clip on the bottom of her and fold her wing tips as described below then guess which way she will fly.

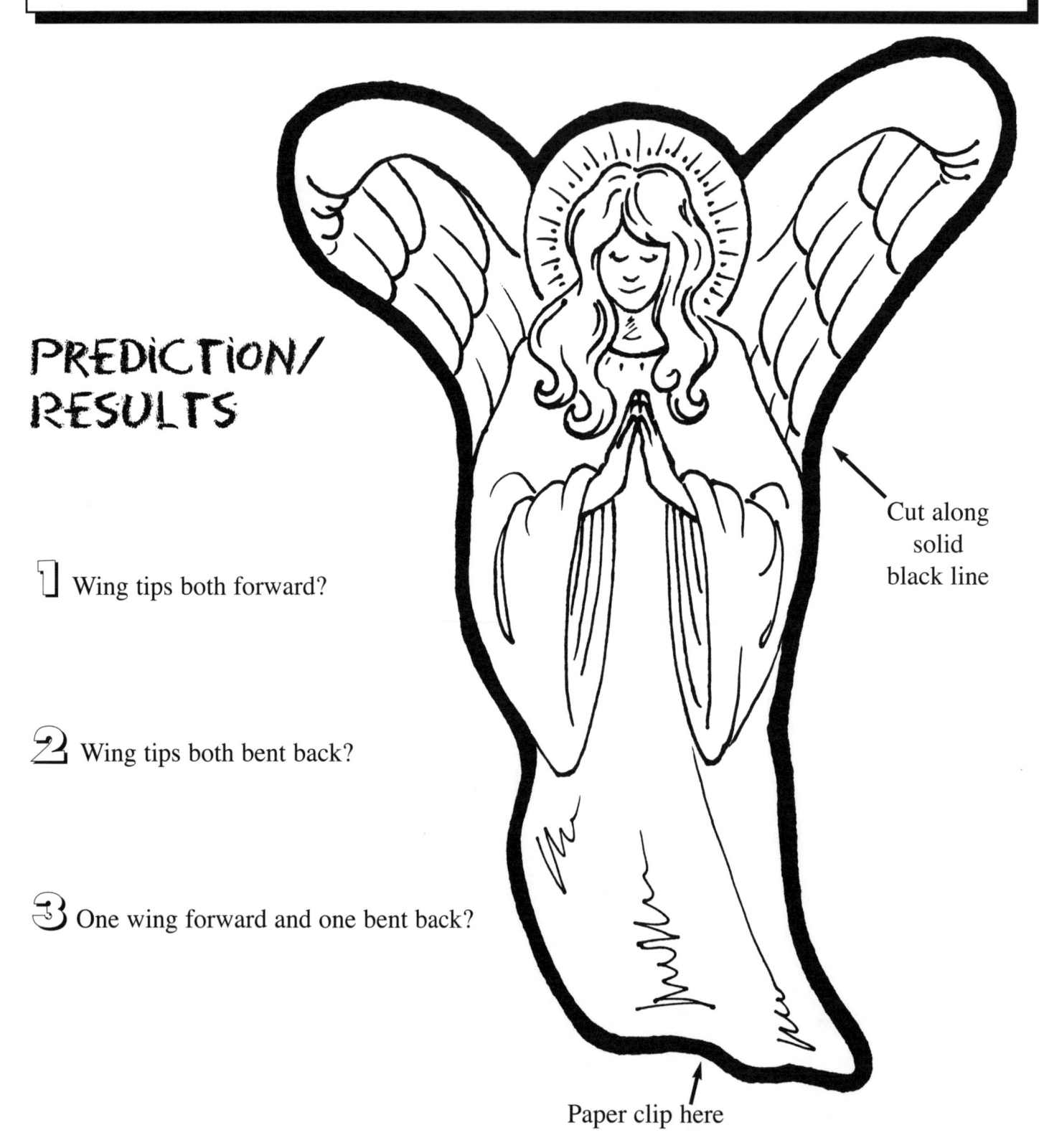

PREDICTION/ RESULTS

1. Wing tips both forward?

2. Wing tips both bent back?

3. One wing forward and one bent back?

Cut along solid black line

Paper clip here

Grades 1 & 2. ©1996 Broadman & Holman, When the Well Runs (Totally and Completely) Dry: Ideas and Activities for Grades 1-6

Look What's in the Stable!

The angels told the shepherds they would find Baby Jesus lying in a manger (Luke 2:8-12). Did you know a manger is where animals eat their hay? There may have been many animals in the stable where Jesus was born. See how easy it is to draw animals, an angel, the star, and Baby Jesus all by yourself? Try to draw as many as you can in the stall above the correct name.

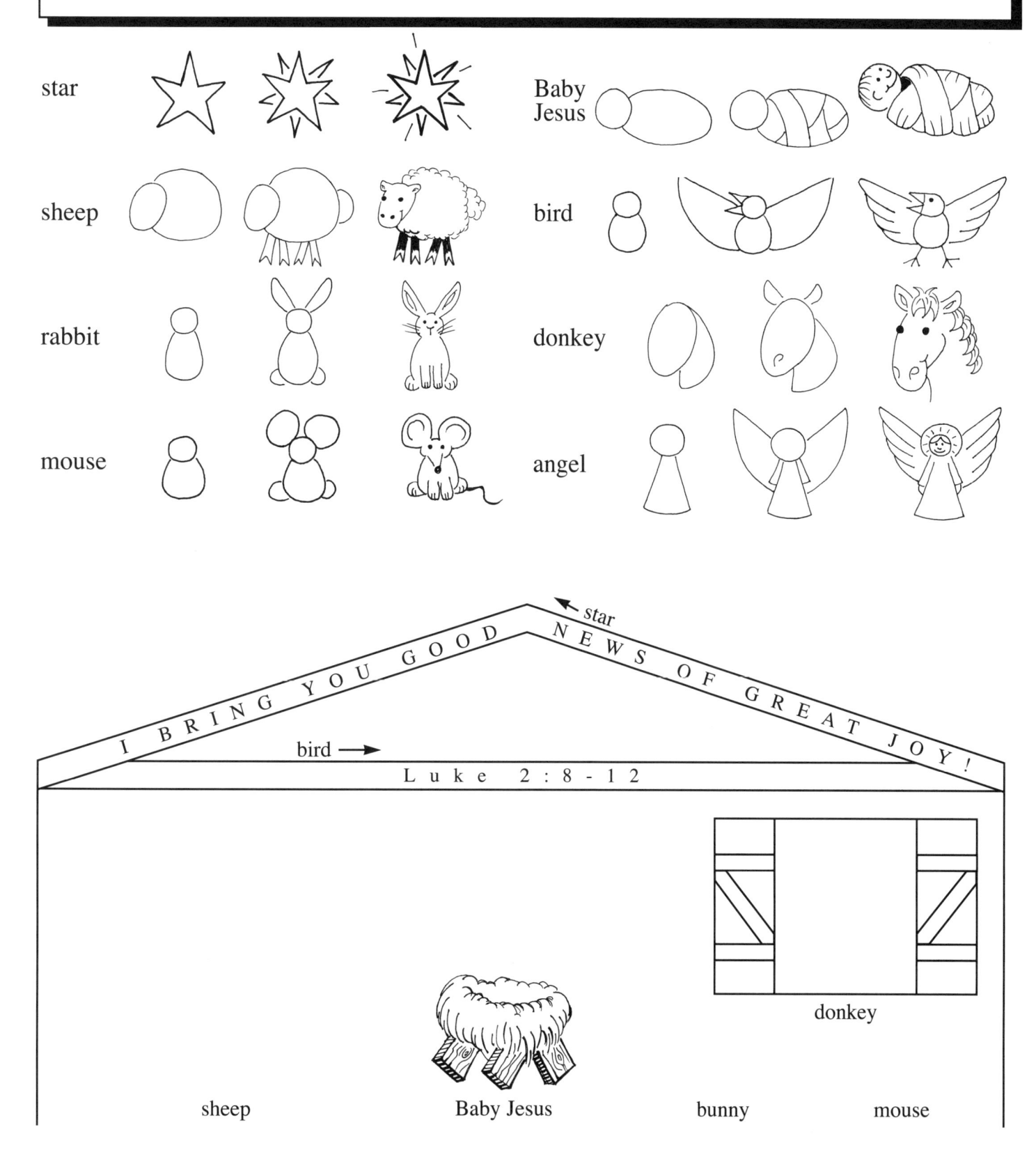

star

Baby Jesus

sheep

bird

rabbit

donkey

mouse

angel

← star

I BRING YOU GOOD NEWS OF GREAT JOY!

bird →

Luke 2:8-12

donkey

sheep   Baby Jesus   bunny   mouse

Grades 1 & 2. ©1996 Broadman & Holman, When the Well Runs (Totally and Completely) Dry: Ideas and Activities for Grades 1-6   9

A Matchless Story!

Match the Christmas scenes on the left with the correct pictures on the right.

LUKE 2:1-20

John the Baptist in Story and Pictures

Read the following story and pictures based on Mark 1:1-11. Color the pictures.

John the Baptist wore [shirt] made of [camel] [hair]. He wore a leather [belt] around his [waist]. He ate [locust]'s and wild [honey]. He said, "Someone is coming more powerful than I. I am not worthy to tie the [laces] on his [sandals]." He baptized Jesus in the Jordan [river]. The [clouds/sky] opened and the Spirit came on Jesus like a [dove]. God told Jesus He [love]'d him. God was [smile/pleased] with His Son.

Grades 1 & 2. ©1996 Broadman & Holman, When the Well Runs (Totally and Completely) Dry: Ideas and Activities for Grades 1-6

A Vase Full of Friends for Jesus

Jesus had many friends that made him feel special. Mary and Martha and Matthew invited him home for dinner. John the Baptist spoke kind words to Jesus and told people everywhere that He was the Son of God. Good friends are like beautiful flowers—they cheer you up and make you feel special.

Color the flowers and the vase with the correct colors. Then you may want to give your picture to a special friend.

1 Red
2 Purple
3 Blue
4 Orange
5 Green
6 Yellow

LUKE 10:38-39   MATTHEW 9:9-10   MARK 1:1-11

Grades 1 & 2. ©1996 Broadman & Holman, When the Well Runs (Totally and Completely) Dry: Ideas and Activities for Grades 1-6

We Have God's Fingerprint!

Genesis 1:27 tells us that we are created in God's image. He made each of us different, but we each have His "fingerprint" on us—because He made us!

To see your own fingerprint, press your finger on an ink pad or rub a pencil real hard, back and forth, in the square. Then rub your finger back and forth across the pencil marking. Next, on the white space, make four or five fingerprints. Using your pencil, decorate your fingerprints and make them into your own creations.

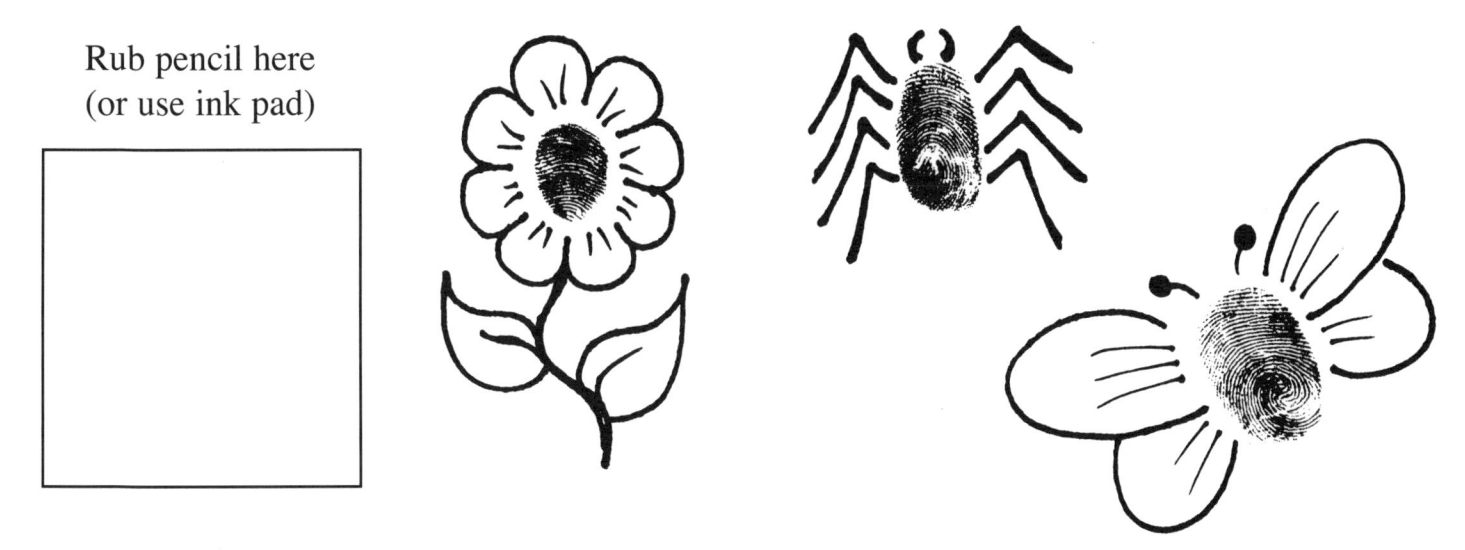

Rub pencil here (or use ink pad)

Put your fingerprints here. Make pictures out of your special fingerprints.

Sharing and Matching Needs

When the church began, most of the Christians shared everything they had with each other: food, houses, land, and money (Acts 4:32-35).

Cut out the cards below and turn them over. Play "match" with them, trying to remember matching pairs. When you get a "match" put the cards in a pile. You may also put your cards together with another friend to make the game more fun.

FOOD	HOUSES	MONEY	LAND
MONEY	LAND	FOOD	HOUSES

14   Grades 1 & 2. ©1996 Broadman & Holman, When the Well Runs (Totally and Completely) Dry: Ideas and Activities for Grades 1-6

Looking for Good News!

Paul and his friends shared the Good News of Jesus with everyone they met. The Bible is full of Good News to share!

Look for 12 hidden Bibles in the picture below and circle them.

LUKE 2:10

Searching for a Joyful Person

"A story with paper and scissors."

God told Jeremiah to look for just one honest person—one good man or woman—and he would forgive the whole city. (Jeremiah 5:1-2)

Below is a story about a search for a joyful, happy friend. You can show and tell this story to others. Practice it today, then try it on someone else and watch them smile!

Once upon a time there was a little boy who wanted nothing more than a happy friend who loved Jesus, too. (Keep paper unfolded: **Figure A**)

He looked in a tent. No friend. (Fold paper in half and hold it upside down like a tent: **Figure B**)

Next he went bicycling up a big round hill and back down again. No friend. (Take a pair of scissors and cut a big half-moon shape: **Figure C**)

Then the little boy decided to climb to the top of an old sharp stump. Again, no friend. (Cut just like the picture in **Figure D**)

The little boy was almost ready to give up. He even peeked inside a tiny little rabbit hole to see if he could find a happy friend. No one was home. He was just about to cry. He was SOOOOO lonely! (Cut little upside down "u" shape as in **Figure E**)

Suddenly the little boy looked up and saw a round window. Of course, he had to go look inside! (Poke hole in paper and cut a round circle as in **Figure F**. Then open up paper to find a happy-faced friend!)

At last, the little boy had found a smiling friend who loved Jesus, too. And they played and played and played all day. That night, just before they went to sleep, they said their prayers and thanked God for good friends.

Figure A

Figure B

Figure C

Figure D

Figure E

Figure F

Color and decorate the "Happy Friend" to make it look like a boy or a girl.

Grades 3 & 4. ©1996 Broadman & Holman, When the Well Runs (Totally and Completely) Dry: Ideas and Activities for Grades 1-6

Jeremiah's Encouraging Letter

What does it mean to encourage someone? Well, Jeremiah was a prophet who had heard some encouraging words from God. He wanted to share them with his people who were discouraged—they were giving up on God because they were being held captive by some mean people called Babylonians. Read Jeremiah 29:4-11 to find out what Jeremiah said to cheer them up. Fill in the blanks of the letter below.

Dear Exiles,

(v. 4) This is what the L___ ___ says, (v.5) "Build _____ and settle down; plant _____ and ___ what they produce. (v. 7) Seek _____ and ___ unto the Lord. (v. 10) In ___ years I will bring you back home. (v. 11) For I know the _____ I have for you, that you will have ___."

Jeremiah

Grades 3 & 4. ©1996 Broadman & Holman, When the Well Runs (Totally and Completely) Dry: Ideas and Activities for Grades 1-6

Finding a Prophet

In the Old Testament, God often spoke through prophets. A prophet was a person who listened to God and then told God's message to the people. Sometimes the messages were hard to hear because the people were disobeying and God had to point that out. When the people kept disobeying, God sometimes had to punish them or they would keep hurting themselves. But He never, never stopped loving them. One of the prophets that had to tell the people a hard-to-hear message is hidden in the message below.

Add the numbers together. Cross out the letters above the addition problems that do NOT add up to nine. Write the prophet's name in the blanks below.

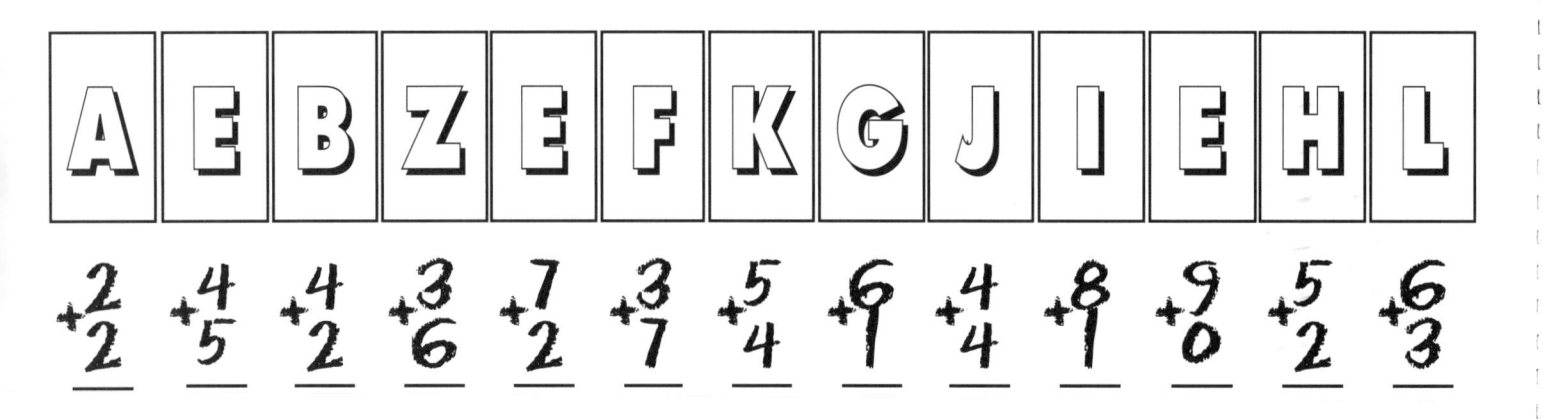

A	E	B	Z	E	F	K	G	J	I	E	H	L
+2/2	+4/5	+4/2	+3/6	+7/2	+3/7	+5/4	+6/1	+4/4	+8/1	+9/0	+5/2	+6/3

___ ___ ___ ___ ___ ___ ___

Do you think it would have been fun to be a prophet? Why or why not?

Flood Factory

Jesus tells a story about foolish and wise choices in Luke 6:46-49. Read the story, then follow the "**FLOOD FACTORY**" instructions to show what a wise person is like and what a foolish person is like.

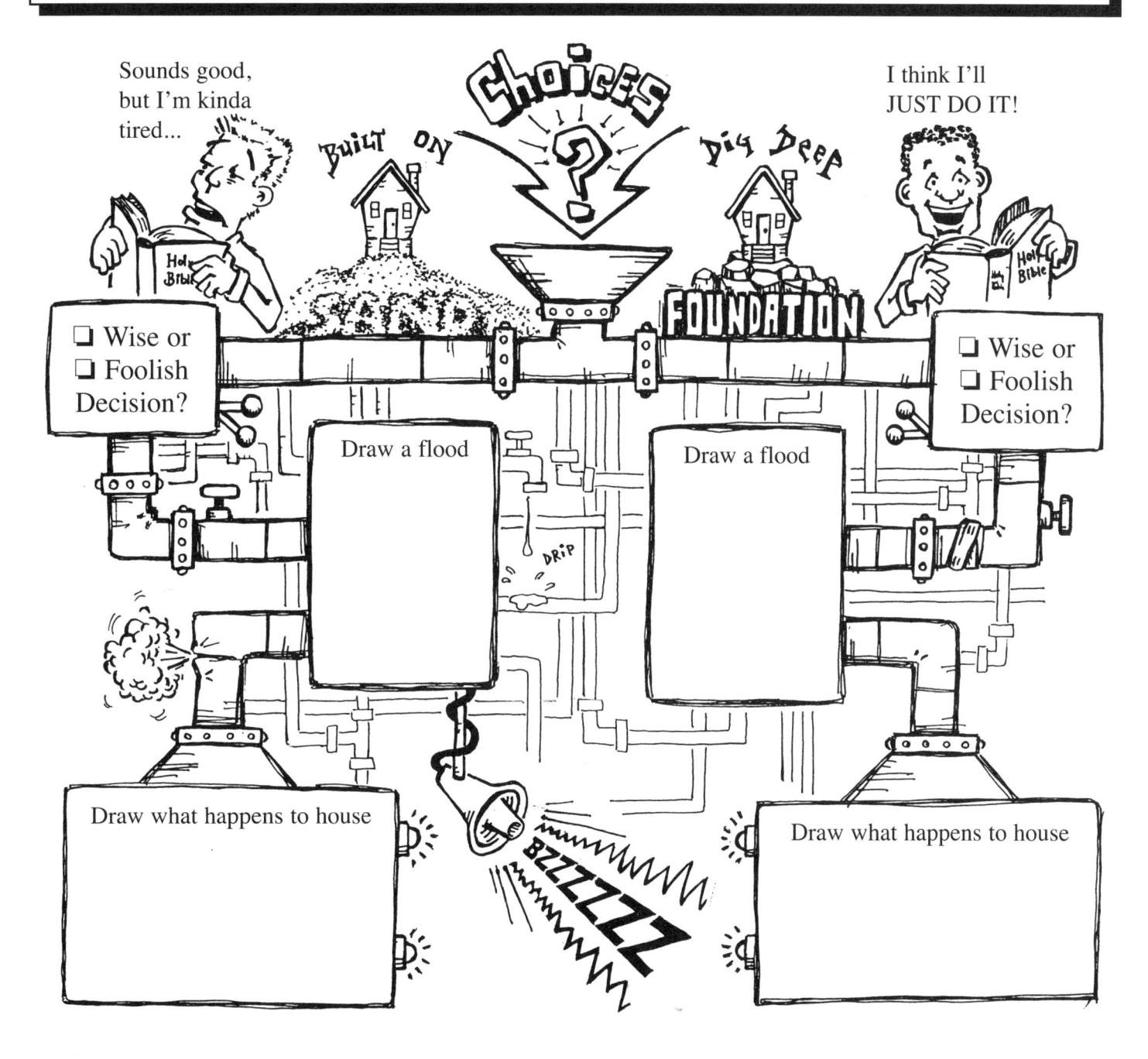

Sounds good, but I'm kinda tired...

BUILT ON

CHOICES?

DIG DEEP

FOUNDATION

I think I'll JUST DO IT!

❏ Wise or
❏ Foolish
Decision?

Draw a flood

Draw a flood

❏ Wise or
❏ Foolish
Decision?

DRIP

BZZZZZZ

Draw what happens to house

Draw what happens to house

"He is like a man who hears my word and _____."

"He is like a man who hears my word and _____."

Share about times when you did something the lazy way and it just fell apart! Give an example of doing something right, even though it was hard, and how you were glad about it later on.

Two Courageous Buddies

The Bible tells an exciting story of two men who believed God at His word, even though the circumstances seemed impossible. Do the puzzles below to discover the names of these friends, then read the story from Numbers 14:6-10.

Cross out the letters that do not equal 5. Write the remaining letters on the blanks.

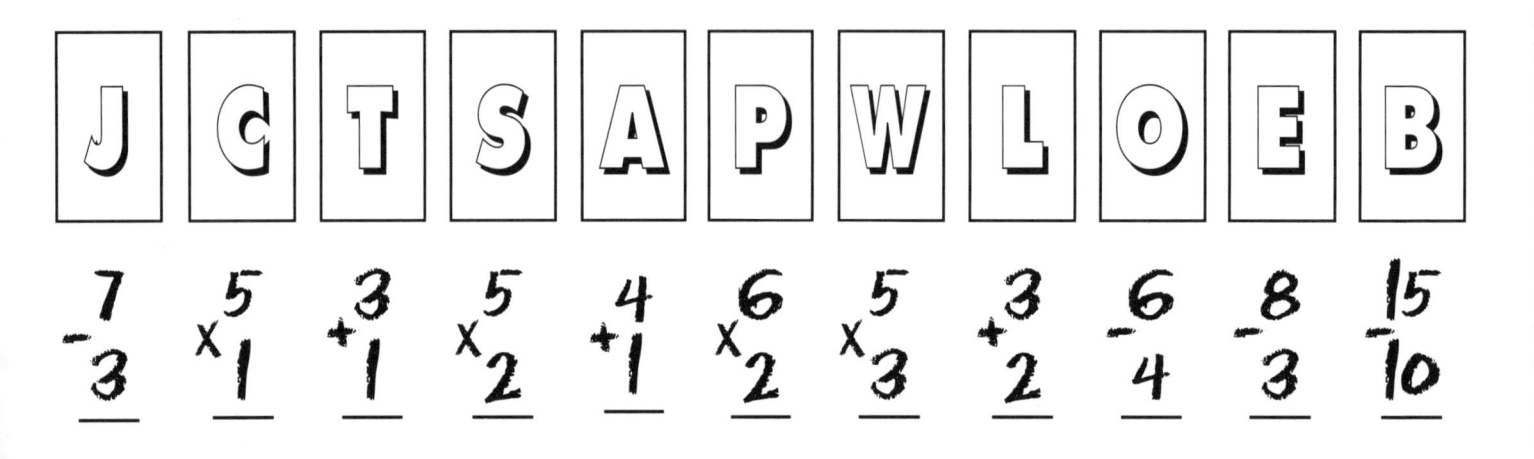

J	C	T	S	A	P	W	L	O	E	B

$\frac{7}{-3}$ $\frac{5}{\times 1}$ $\frac{3}{+1}$ $\frac{5}{\times 2}$ $\frac{4}{+1}$ $\frac{6}{\times 2}$ $\frac{5}{\times 3}$ $\frac{3}{+2}$ $\frac{6}{-4}$ $\frac{8}{-3}$ $\frac{15}{-10}$

___ ___ ___ ___ ___

A	J	O	S	H	U	A	A	J
U	O	O	P	Z	A	D	U	O
H	S	X	S	F	C	L	H	S
S	H	P	E	H	U	B	S	H
O	U	A	U	D	U	M	O	U
J	A	Z	D	K	L	A	J	A

How many times can you find the name "Joshua"? _____

20   Grades 3 & 4. ©1996 Broadman & Holman, When the Well Runs (Totally and Completely) Dry: Ideas and Activities for Grades 1-6

Hidden Treasure in Canaan

Joshua and Caleb urged the Israelites to go into the Land of Canaan, "a land flowing with milk and honey." They saw grapes and figs and pomegranates that were as big as they were! But the people were afraid of the giants in the land. God wants to give us good gifts, but we must trust Him to give us strength to overcome our fears.

Look for the following items in the picture below:

milk (3)   honey (2)   grapes (2)   figs (2)   pomegranates (3)

Land of Canaan

A Cornucopia of Blessings!

It is a good think to give thanks unto the Lord. Psalm 92:1

THANKSGIVING

How many words can you make out of "Thanksgiving" in 2 minutes? Write them below:

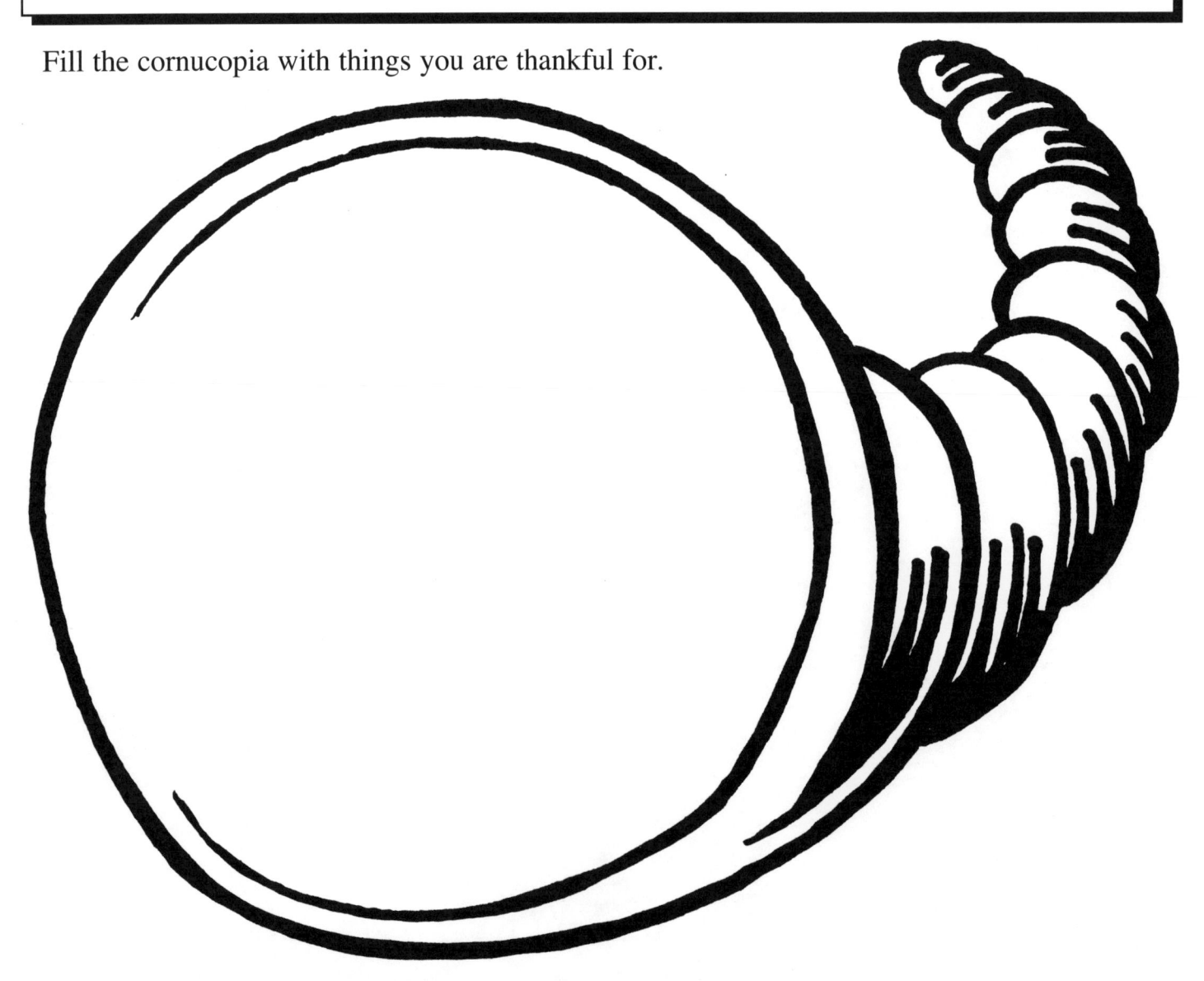

Fill the cornucopia with things you are thankful for.

BOOKS OF THE OLD TESTAMENT

Genesis
Exodus
Leviticus
Numbers
Deuteronomy
Joshua
Judges
Ruth
1 Samuel
2 Samuel
1 Kings
2 Kings
1 Chronicles
2 Chronicles
Ezra
Nehemiah
Esther
Job
Psalms
Proverbs

Ecclesiastes
Song of Solomon
Isaiah
Jeremiah
Lamentations
Ezekiel
Daniel
Hosea
Joel
Amos
Obadiah
Jonah
Micah
Nahum
Habakkuk
Zephaniah
Haggai
Zechariah
Malachi

BOOKS OF THE NEW TESTAMENT

Matthew	1 Timothy
Mark	2 Timothy
Luke	Titus
John	Philemon
Acts	Hebrews
Romans	James
1 Corinthians	1 Peter
2 Corinthians	2 Peter
Galatians	1 John
Ephesians	2 John
Philippians	3 John
Colossians	Jude
1 Thessalonians	Revelation
2 Thessalonians	

Musical Thanksgiving!

Psalm 98 tells us of all things that will make musical praise to God—even things in nature will praise God with song someday! Read Psalm 98:4-9 to help you work the crossword puzzle below.

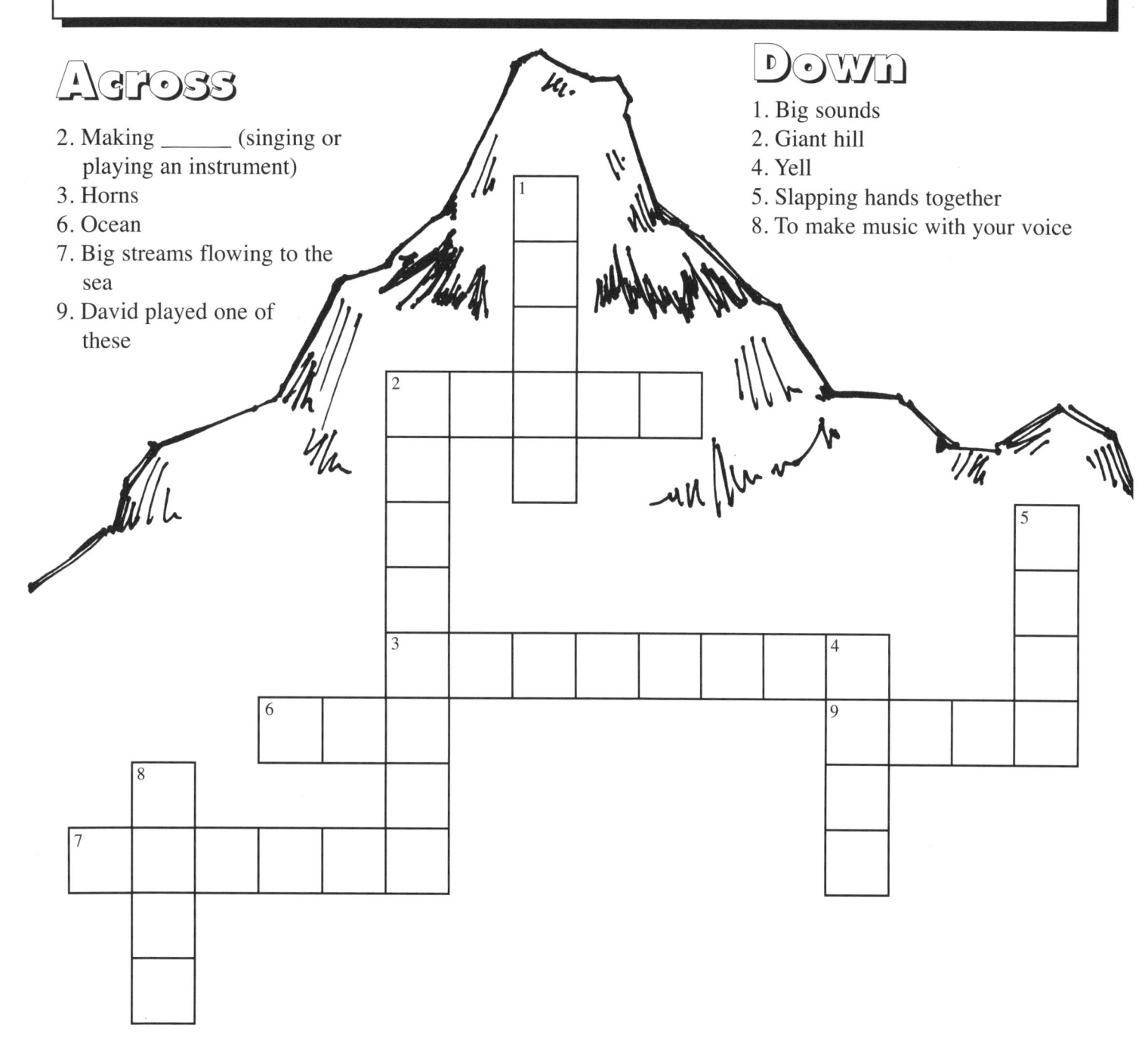

Across

2. Making _____ (singing or playing an instrument)
3. Horns
6. Ocean
7. Big streams flowing to the sea
9. David played one of these

Down

1. Big sounds
2. Giant hill
4. Yell
5. Slapping hands together
8. To make music with your voice

**LET THE MOUNTAINS SING TOGETHER FOR JOY.
PSALM 98:8, NIV**

A Son Comes Home!

Luke 15:11-24 tells the story of a son who ran away from home, only to find he was miserable. He came back to his father's house and was welcomed with open arms. Help the son find his way back to the father. Then read the story and draw pictures along the path of some of the things that happened in story.

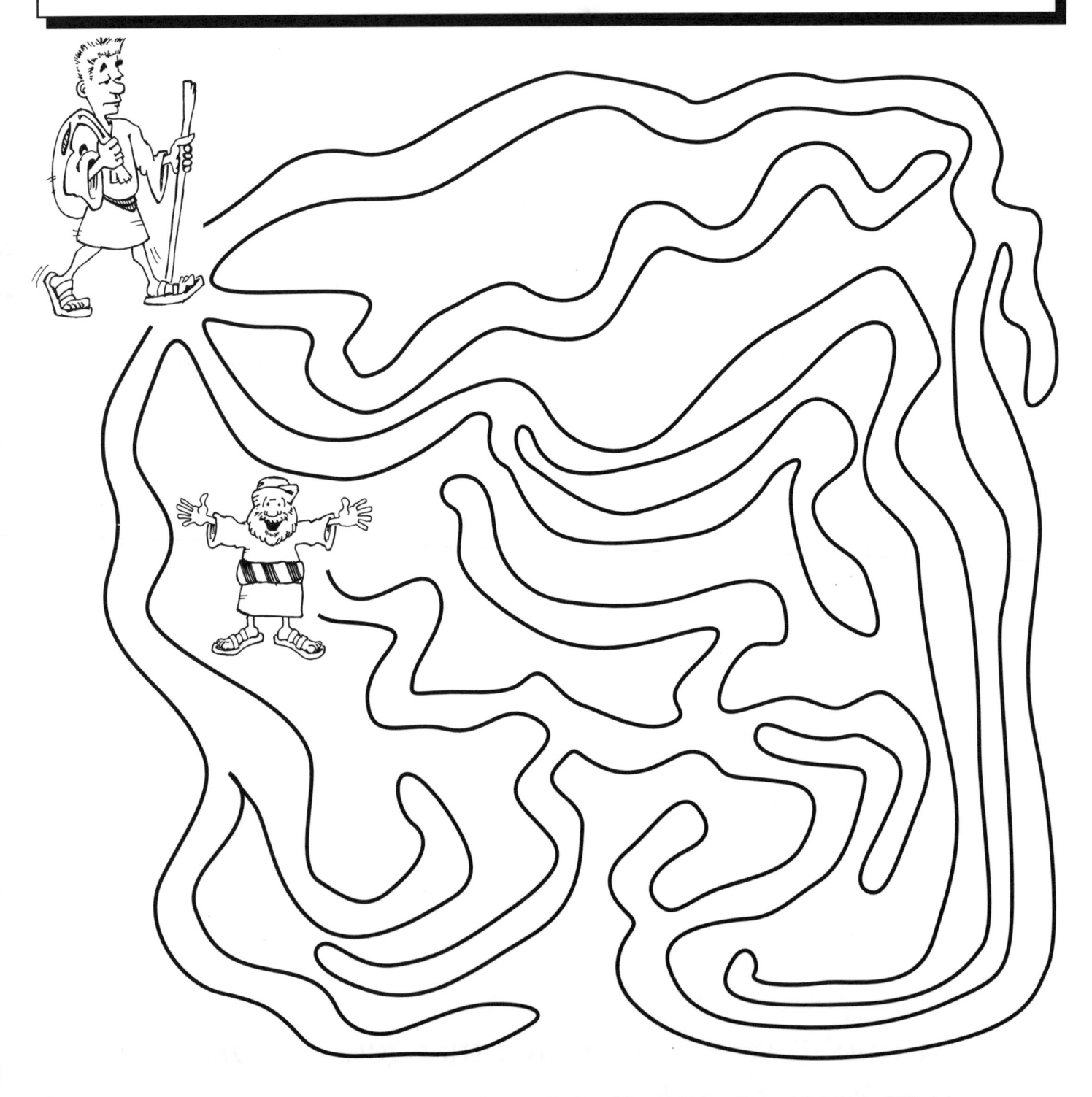

Happy Picture Writing

People of long ago sometimes used pictures, or hieroglyphics, instead of words to write their messages. Use the symbols to write the phrases below. If there is not a symbol for the word you need, you may go ahead and write out the word.

Bring	Great Joy	Good	News
I	Baby	Cloths	Lying
Manger	You	Find	Wrapped

I bring you good news of great joy.
You will find the baby lying in a manger.

LUKE 2:10-12

Celebrate His Birthday!

As you know, this is the time of year when we celebrate Jesus' birthday. So you get to plan His party!

Fill in the guest list with names of people in the Bible that helped celebrate the birth of Jesus. Then draw a present that you would have like to have given Baby Jesus. Finally, decorate a birthday cake that you think Jesus would enjoy. (Don't forget to write a birthday message on the cake!)

Guest List

1.
2.
3.
4.
5.

Who came to honor Jesus?

What gift would you bring to Baby Jesus?

Decorate a birthday cake for Jesus.

LUKE 2:4-5, 9, 15   MATTHEW 2:1

A Royal Search

Starting at Point 1A, connect the dots in numerical and/or alphabetical order. Then, using the clues from the dot-to-dots, write the letter that goes with the correct number above the numbered blanks. Read from Matthew 2:1-2 to help you finish filling in the rest of the blanks above the "jewels." Now what does it say all together?

For the crowning touch, color, cut out, and wear your picture!

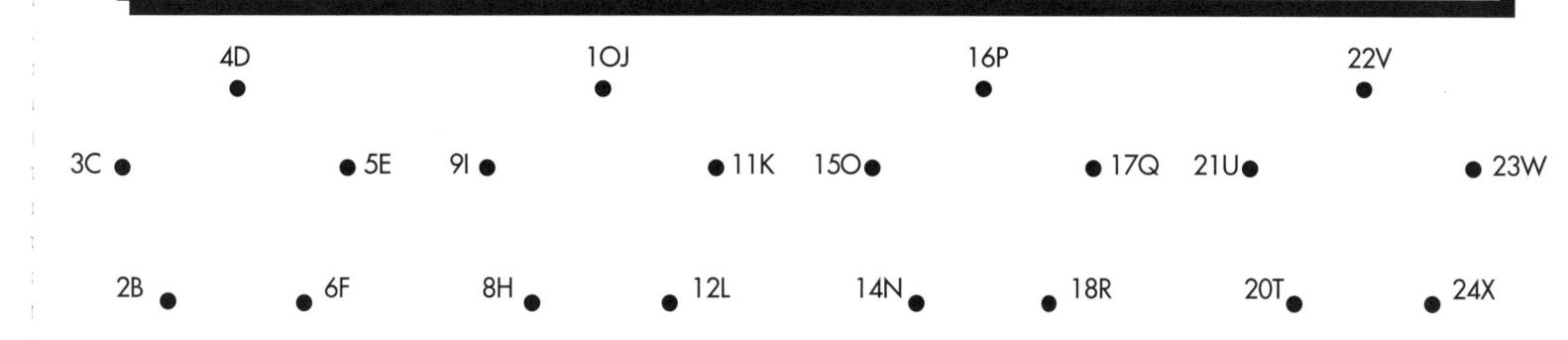

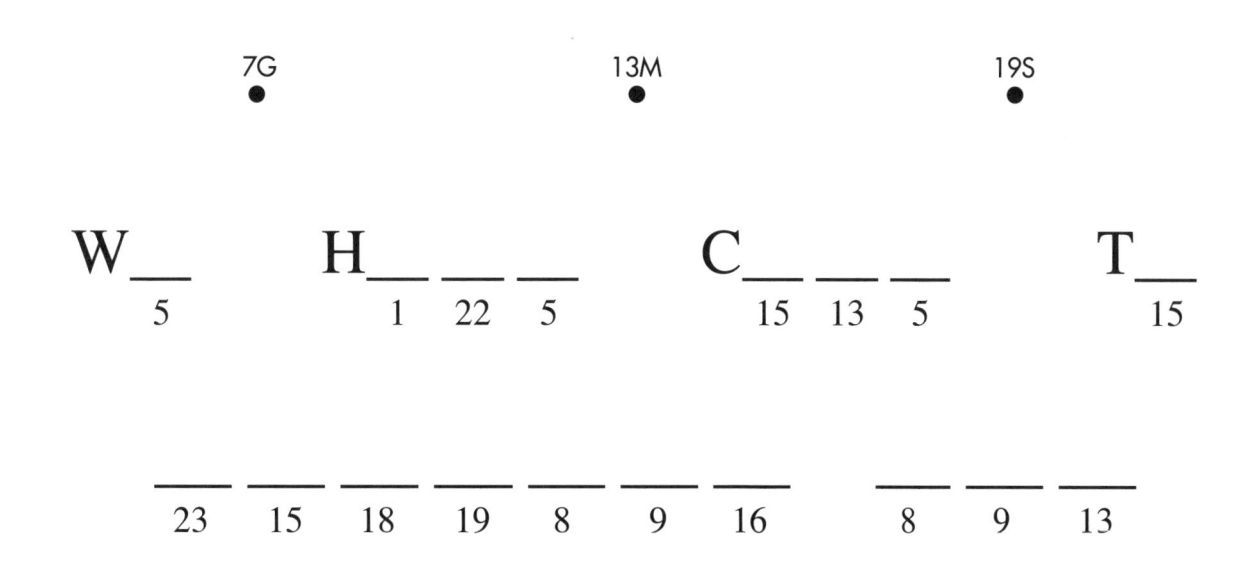

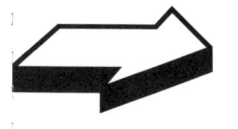

```
    4D            10J           16P           22V
 3C    5E    9I     11K  15O      17Q  21U      23W
 2B     6F    8H      12L    14N     18R    20T    24X



              7G            13M          19S


       W __      H __ __ __      C __ __ __      T __
          5         1  22  5       15  13  5        15


        __ __ __ __ __ __ __     __ __ __
        23 15 18 19  8  9 16      8  9 13


 1A                                                    25Y
    26Z
```

NOTE TO TEACHER: Attach 1" by 18" strips of paper to the crowns by adjusting them to fit the children and stapling.

"I Am Unique" Cartoon Strip

Genesis 1:27 says that God created us "in His image." Though God is much, much greater than man, we do share some of His personality. God gave us five senses with which to understand the world around us. Each person likes to see, hear, taste, touch, and smell different things—this is one way that we are unique, or special.

Finish the cartoon strips below by drawing and describing the things you like best.

Hi! My name is	I like to taste	I love to see
My favorite thing to touch is	Mmm! I love the smell of	Can you hear the

I am thankful for _____.

Gifts for Special Friends

Jesus had some special friends: John the Baptist, Mary, Martha, and Matthew to name a few. Do you have some special friends? What do you like about them the most?

Write the name of a special friend (they can be family members, too) on each of the bookmarks below. Then draw and decorate the bookmark for them. Put pictures of things you know your friend likes to do or words that describe him or her on the bookmark. Give them the bookmark as a present.

LUKE 10:38-39   MATTHEW 9:9-10   MARK 1:1-11

Helpers Are Great!

When the church first started, everyone helped each other. You may remember that Stephen helped take care of the widows so that the missionaries could go and share the gospel in far off places. People shared food, money, and chores just the way you do in your family.

Below are some ways you can help around the house. Draw a line from the words on the left to the correct words on the right.

1. Wash the
2. Run an
3. Cook
4. Watch
5. Pick-up
6. Walk
7. Hug
8. Sweep
9. Bake
10. Draw

a. cookies
b. the baby
c. the dog
d. car
e. your mom or dad
f. errand
g. the floor
h. breakfast
i. a picture
j. your clothes

The Faithful Life and Death of Stephen

In the book of Acts, we read about a man "full of the Spirit" named Stephen. Try to put the events of Stephen's life in order. If you need help, you will find clues in Acts 6:1-5, 8, 11; 7:2, 56, 59-60. (Look over all of Chapter 7 to see how L-O-O-O-O-O-O-O-N-G Stephen spoke!)

☐ Stephen is falsely accused.

☐ Stephen does miracles.

☐ Stephen chosen to help widows.

☐ Stephen gives long speech.

☐ Stephen forgives people as they stone him.

☐ Stephen see heavens open.

Searching for a Few Good Men (and Women)

The Lord told Jeremiah to search and search to see if he could find just ONE honest, truthful person and God would forgive the whole city (Jeremiah 5:1-2). the power of one person is awesome!

Match the names of the following people in the Bible who stood for right in a world gone wrong. Then find their names in the word search (be sure to look forward, backwards, and sideways).

Daniel	Queen whose courage saved a life
Noah	Faithful to god when tempted, forgave his brothers
Abraham	Thrown to lions for not bowing to other gods
Caleb & Joshua	Followed God to faraway land called Ur
Esther	Woman who helped spies escape from evil city
Rahab	Stayed and took care of mother-in-law, Naomi
Ruth	Thrown in fiery furnace for not worshipping idols
Shadrach, Meshach, and Abednego	Believed they could defeat giants in land
Hezekiah	Obeyed God—his family was saved from the flood
Joseph	King who followed God

V	T	N	R	S	B	G	H	Z	A
U	N	Q	O	A	F	E	D	B	K
O	D	C	H	A	O	N	M	C	J
M	P	A	B	E	D	N	E	G	O
A	R	L	N	O	W	X	S	R	S
H	I	E	O	I	Y	A	H	U	H
A	J	B	K	T	E	E	A	T	U
R	E	H	T	S	E	L	C	H	A
B	H	C	A	R	D	A	H	S	L
A	H	E	Z	E	K	I	A	H	M
W	Z	P	J	O	S	E	P	H	O

Messages in Braille (that will never fail!)

People who have lost their sight have to rely on the sense of touch to help them "see." When times are hard, sometimes we "lose our sight" of God's promises. Jeremiah wrote a letter to encourage his friends being held captive in Babylon to "look" forward with the "eyes of faith" to the good things God promised them.

Below are number in Braille. Practice seeing if you can "read" the Braille numbers without looking at the number underneath. You may want to use a sharp pencil or pen to poke small holes in the dots so you can practice "reading" by touch.

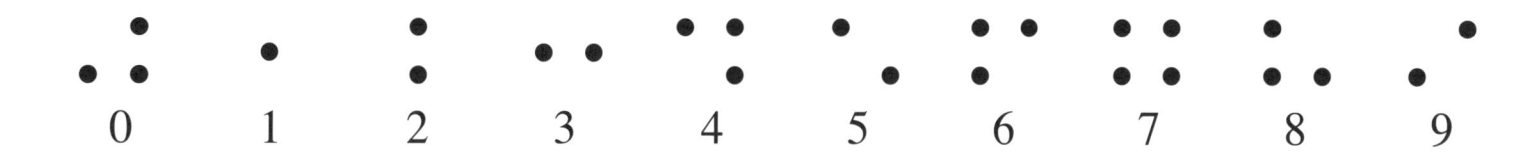

0   1   2   3   4   5   6   7   8   9

Fold this paper in half, along the line, to hide the Braille-number clues above and see if you can "read" the Braille dots from memory. Using the NumberLetter key for each puzzle below, find the letter that goes with each Braille number and finish the following promises.

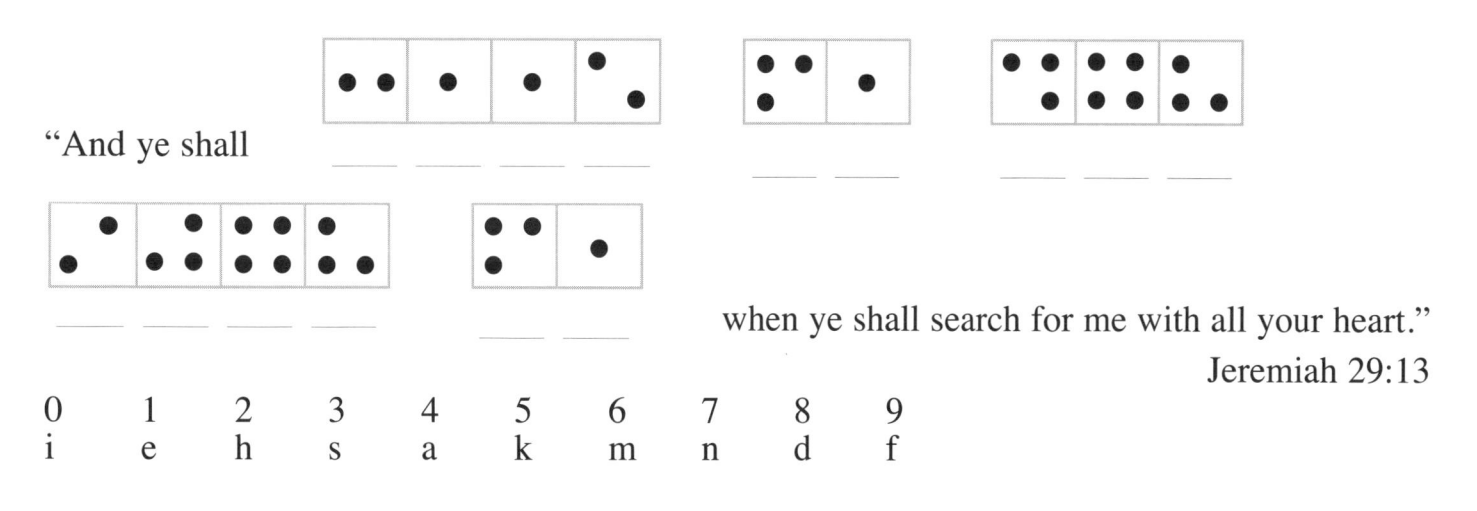

"And ye shall ___ ___ ___ ___   ___ ___   ___ ___ ___

___ ___ ___ ___   ___ ___   when ye shall search for me with all your heart."

Jeremiah 29:13

0	1	2	3	4	5	6	7	8	9
i	e	h	s	a	k	m	n	d	f

"For I know the thoughts that I think toward you, saith the Lord,

___ ___ ___ ___ ___ ___ ___ ___ of ___ ___ ___ ___ ___ and not of evil...."

Jeremiah 29:11.

0	1	2	3	4	5	6	7	8	9
c	s	t	p	h	e	o	a	u	g

Following Instructions

Prophets had to listen very carefully to specific instructions from God. Carefully follow the instructions below to find the correct letter for each number. Put all the letters together and you will find a phrase that God often repeated to Ezekiel to give him courage to obey.

___ ___   ___ ___ ___   ___ ___   ___ ___ ___ ___ ___ ___
1   2   3   4   5   6   7   8   9   10 11 12 13

1 First letter in the name of man who was thrown in lion's den

2 Fifteenth letter of alphabet

3 This letter sounds like the place where "there was not room" for Mary and Joseph

4 Letter shaped like a donut

5 This letter sounds like a common hot or cold drink

6 This letter sounds like an insect that packs a stinger

7 Two letters past "c" in the alphabet

8 Letter that looks like a tee pee

9 Tenth letter of the alphabet counting BACKWARDS from "p" (don't count "p")

10 Sounds like the word that goes in the following sentence: Where ____ you going?

11 Letter the rhymes with "may"

12 Sounds like something on your face that blinks

13 You do not want this letter on a report card

34   Grades 5 & 6. ©1996 Broadman & Holman, When the Well Runs (Totally and Completely) Dry: Ideas and Activities for Grades 1-6

Wise Man, Foolish Man - What's the Difference?

You know what happened when the foolish man built his house on the sand and the wise man built his on the rock. When the floods came - talk about different results!

Now look at the picture on the right. Then look carefully at the picture on the left and find thirteen differences.

Answer Key

Different style chimneys on Wise man's house. • Doorknobs on Wise man's house are on different sides. • Wise man's window is up on right, down on left. • Extra plank sticking out of sand on the left. • Wise man's house on left has a path to the door instead of steps. • Foolish man's "For Sale" sign is missing on the left. • Flower by Wise man's house is missing on left. • No bird on Foolish man's roof on the left. • Extra sand dune by Foolish man's house on the left. • Wise man's house on left is brick, wood on right. • Wise man on left is barefooted. • Broken window sticking out of the sand is missing on right. • Water puddle under Foolish man's house is missing on right.

Grades 5 & 6. ©1996 Broadman & Holman, When the Well Runs (Totally and Completely) Dry: Ideas and Activities for Grades 1-6

Recipe for a Grateful Heart

Thanksgiving is a time of fun, family, food, and (of course) giving thanks! Write a "recipe" for a Grateful Heart in the recipe card below.

1. Name your original "recipe."
2. List 10 ingredients for a Happy Thanksgiving. (They might be love, family, prayer, Aunt Betsy's pecan pie - anything that makes Thanksgiving Day special to you.)
3. Write instructions for putting your thanksgiving "ingredients" together. You may want to use some of the following "cooking words" in your recipe: mix, blend, whirl, roll, warm-up, cool, pat, fold in, add, separate. Have fun with this—it is okay to be funny. One thing we are thankful for is the gift of laughter!

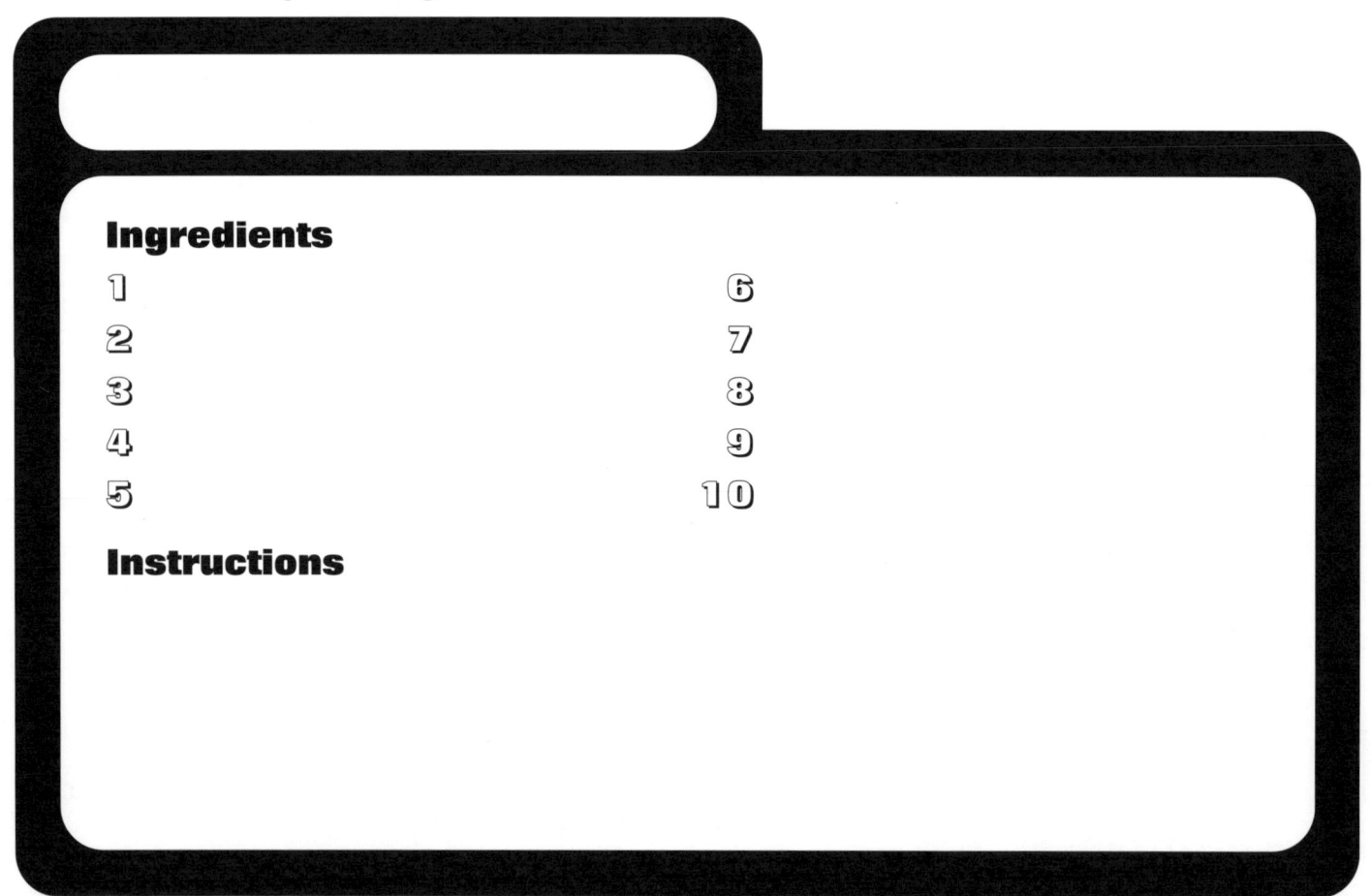

Ingredients
1.
2.
3.
4.
5.
6.
7.
8.
9.
10.

Instructions

On the back, draw a picture of what your perfect "Thanksgiving Day" would look like if everyone followed your "recipe."

IT IS A GOOD THING TO GIVE THANKS UNTO THE LORD. PSALM 92:1

Filling in Forgiveness

There is a wonderful story in the Bible about a father's forgiveness. It is found in Luke 15:11-24. Many of the words form the story are listed below. Fill in the blanks to complete the words. Then transfer the letter to the correct number in the "mystery phrase" to find what we call this story today. (#1 is done for you)

1 F A̲ T H E R
2 P _ G
3 W E A _ T H
4 _ R O P E R T Y
5 F O U N _

$\overline{14}\ \overline{17}\ \overline{15}\ \overline{13}\ \overline{18}\ \overline{12}\ \overline{16}$

6 _ O B E
7 R I N _
8 L _ S T
9 F E A _ T

$\overline{19}\ \overline{20}$

10 S I _ N E D
11 W _ R T H Y
12 S A N D _ E S
13 F _ M I N E

$\overline{4}\ \overline{6}\ \overline{8}\ \overline{5}\ \overline{2}\ \overline{7}\ \overline{1}^{A}\ \overline{3}$

14 _ O D S
15 H I _ E D
16 M _ N
17 C O M P _ S S I O N

$\overline{9}\ \overline{11}\ \overline{10}$

18 C E L E _ R A T E
19 B R _ T H E R
20 _ A T T E D

The "Good News" News

Pretend you are a newspaper journalist and write about what happened to Zechariah and Elizabeth. Look up the scripture by each column to help you answer the questions and fill in the blanks. When you get to the "Birth Announcement" draw a picture that describes what happened in the verses beside it. Make up a catchy headline when you finish.

Headline (Make Up Last, After Blanks Are Filled In)

Zechariah & Elizabeth

BIO
Zechariah:

Occupation _____

When? _____

Elizabeth:

Whose descendant? _____
_____

Any children? _____

Why? _____

Ages of "Zech" & "Liz"
_____

PERSONALITIES?

Luke 1:5-7

Angel's Message #1

"Don't be _____."

"Name him _____."

"He will be _____ to you."

What will He do for Israel?

"He will turn hearts of _____ to their _____."

Luke 1:13-17

Angel's Message #2

"I was sent to speak G_____ N_____."

"Now you will ___ _____ till _____."

How Long? _____

Luke 1:19-21

BIRTH ANNOUNCEMENT

"   "

Photo Caption   Luke 1:57-64

38 Grades 5 & 6. ©1996 Broadman & Holman, When the Well Runs (Totally and Completely) Dry: Ideas and Activities for Grades 1-6

Christmas Jigsaw Drawing

Instructions: Look for square number one in the top picture and try to draw the same lines and curves into square number one in the bottom puzzle. Continue drawing each square 2-36 into the bottom puzzle. A Christmas picture and message will soon appear.

Grades 5 & 6. ©1996 Broadman & Holman, When the Well Runs (Totally and Completely) Dry: Ideas and Activities for Grades 1-6

Jesus and John Cross Paths

In Mark 1:1-11, we find the story of Jesus and His cousin John crossing paths. Read the story, then fill in the "dove" crossword puzzle.

ACROSS
1. God's voice came out of _____
2. John was _____ people in the river
6. John also ate these insects for protein
7. Who was John's cousin and the Son of God?

DOWN
1. John ate this sweet, sticky stuff
3. The _____ descended on Jesus
4. John baptized Jesus in this
5. The Spirit looked like a ____

Five Letter Flower Power

Write the answers to the clues in the flower (going from the outside to the middle). The first one is done for you. When you are finished, read around the outside of the flower to discover a message from Luke 10:38-42

1. Floating baby in basket
2. Spoke for Moses
3. Woman who helped spies escape evil city
4. Not old, but _____
5. Jesus said to come to him as a _____
6. We are to love God will all our _____
7. "Have no _____ gods before me."
8. "I am the Alpha and _____." (Revelation 1:8)
9. This blocked the entrance to Jesus' tomb
10. Satan is our _____
11. We are to forgive seventy times _____ (Matthew 18:22)
12. Jonah was in the whale's belly this many days and nights
13. The wise man built this on a rock
14. In the beginning God made the heavens and the _____
15. Jesus said man cannot live by this alone
16. Moses led his people out of this country
17. Peter used this to cut off a guard's ear
18. Jesus told Martha only one _____ was needed

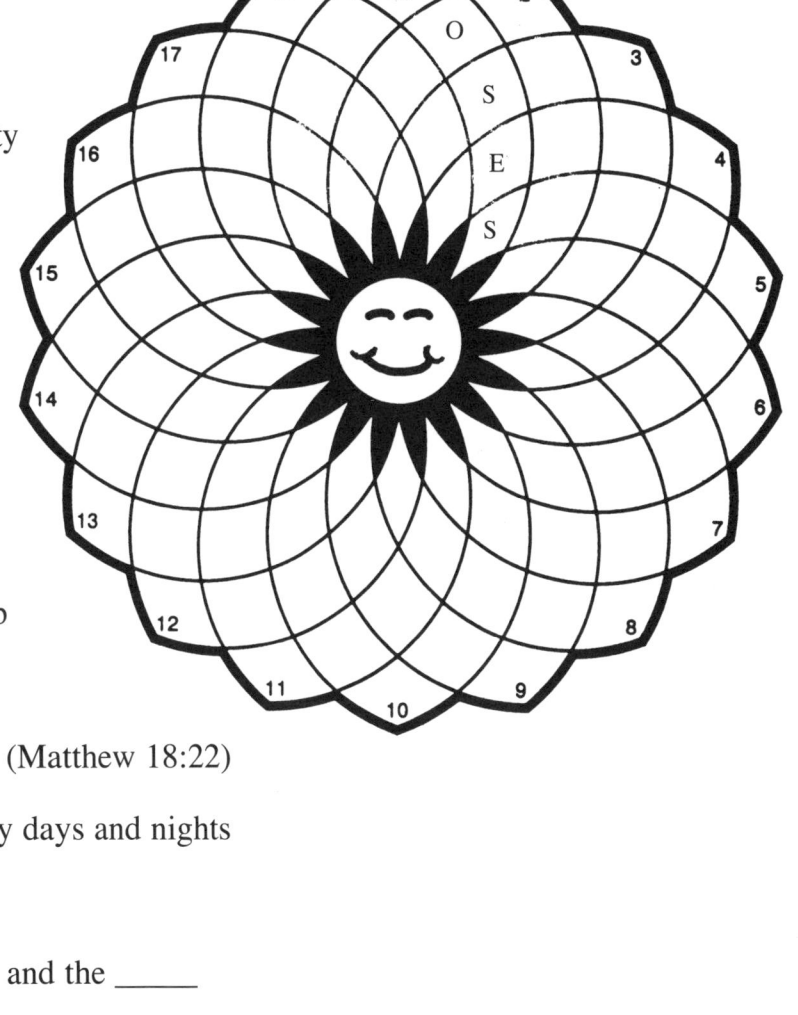

WHAT WAS THE "BEST THING" THAT MARY CHOSE?

Acrosti-Clue

Answer the following questions of fill-in-the blanks. Then read the letters in the squares and you will find the occupation of someone who invited Jesus and his friends to dinner.

1. Paul chose this young man as a helper (Acts 16:1-3)   1. ☐ _ _ _ _ _ _
2. Paul and Barnabas were sent to this city (Acts 15:22)   2. ☐ _ _ _ _ _ _
3. "I will _____ you, O Lord." Psalm 30   3. _ ☐ _ _ _
4. Another name for Jesus   4. ☐ _ _ _ _
5. "_____ our eyes, Lord"   5. ☐ _ _ _
6. A physician, he wrote the book of Acts   6. ☐ _ _ _
7. Christians are to ____ one another   7. ☐ _ _ _
8. First garden in the Bible   8. ☐ _ _ _
9. God _____us in all our troubles (2 Corinthians 1:4)   9. ☐ _ _ _ _ _ _
10. New Testament book, comes just before Philemon   10. ☐ _ _ _ _ _
11. A run-away slave, Paul loved him like a brother (Philemon 1:10-16)   11. ☐ _ _ _ _ _ _ _ _
12. In ancient Israel, this was a family member who bought a slave's way to freedom. Jesus is this to us! (See Job 19:25)   12. ☐ _ _ _ _ _ _ _

A. What is the occupation of the man who invited Jesus and his disciples for dinner?
_____ (Mark 2:13-17)

B. What did Jesus tell the people who accused him of eating with such "sinners?"
_____ (Mark 2:17)

42   Grades 5 & 6. ©1996 Broadman & Holman, When the Well Runs (Totally and Completely) Dry: Ideas and Activities for Grades 1-6

Spreading the Gospel Around and Around!

In the book of Acts, everywhere missionaries went they spread the Good News about Christ and how to live a life of love. In the puzzle below, answer the questions and fill in the circles. You will find some of the messages the missionaries shared (and the name of one of the missionaries). IMPORTANT: Be sure to write the word in the direction of the arrow!

1. Matthew 11:28   Jesus promises to give ___ ___ ___ ___
2. Matthew 28:7   Go ___ ___ ___ ___ that Jesus is risen!
3. Ephesians 5:2   Walk in ___ ___ ___ ___
4. Galatians 6:16 Peace and mercy to all who follow this ___ ___ ___ ___ (that we become new creations in Christ)
5. Galatians 6:8   We will ___ ___ ___ ___ if we please the Spirit
6. Who wrote the letters to the Galatians and the Ephesians? ___ ___ ___ ___

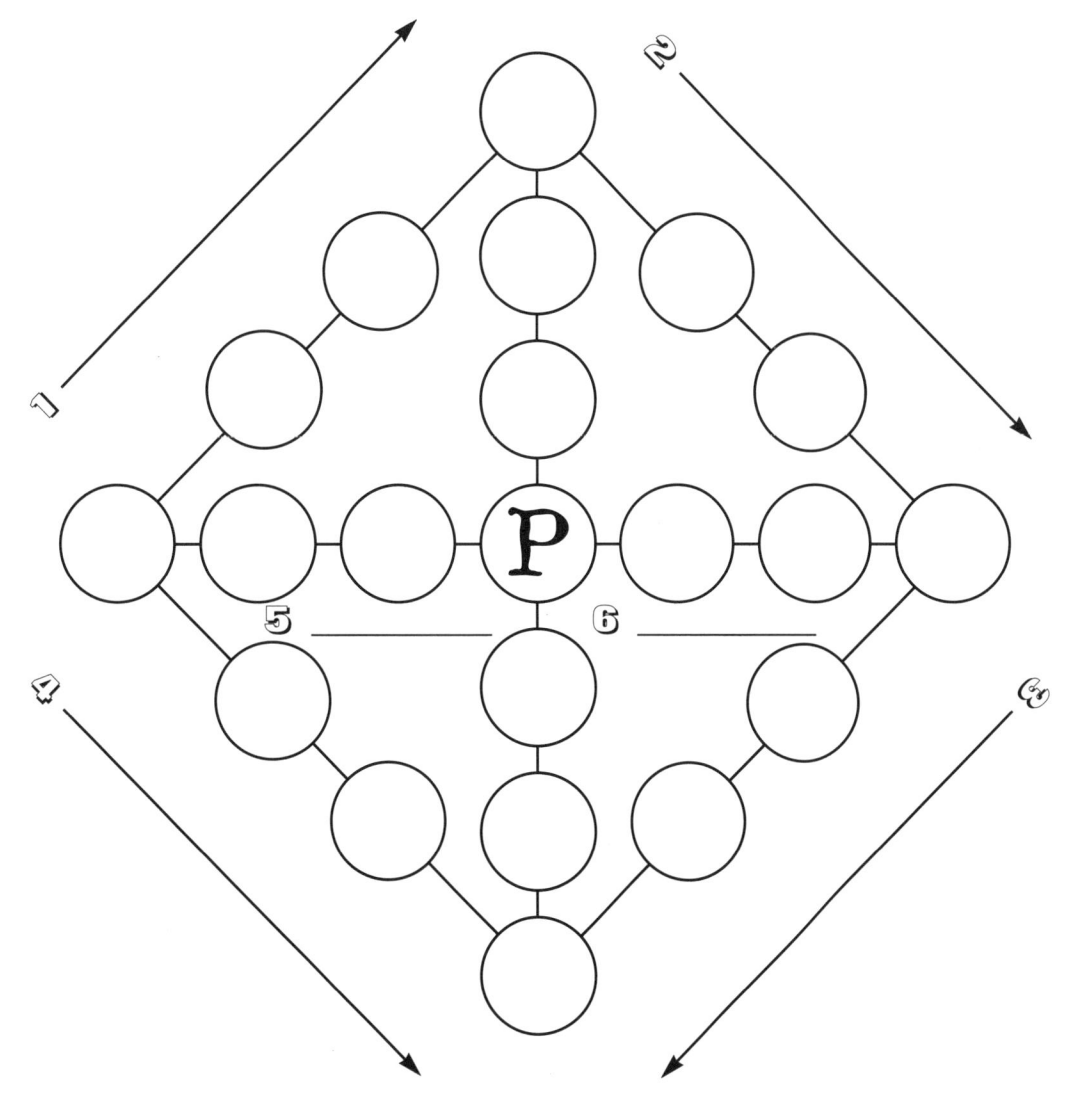

Ring Around the Book of Acts

Imagine that each set of the rings below can turn and spin. In your head, turn them until all the letters line up to create words. (The words will read from the outside ring to the inside ring.) Write each letter in the blanks as you line them up to discover the names of missionaries and their messages. If you have trouble doing this in your head, carefully cut out each ring along the lines, then rotate them until you spell out the words!

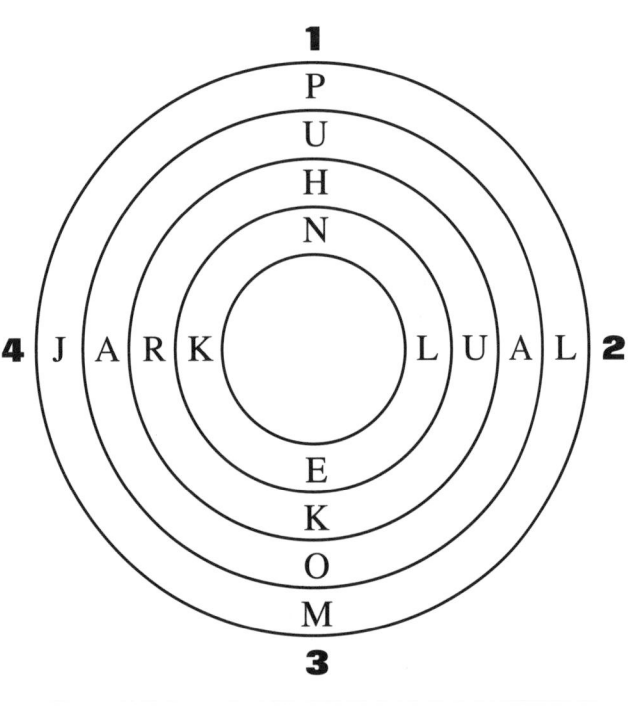

Missionaries

1 _ _ _ _ _

2 _ _ _ _ _

3 _ _ _ _ _

4 _ _ _ _ _

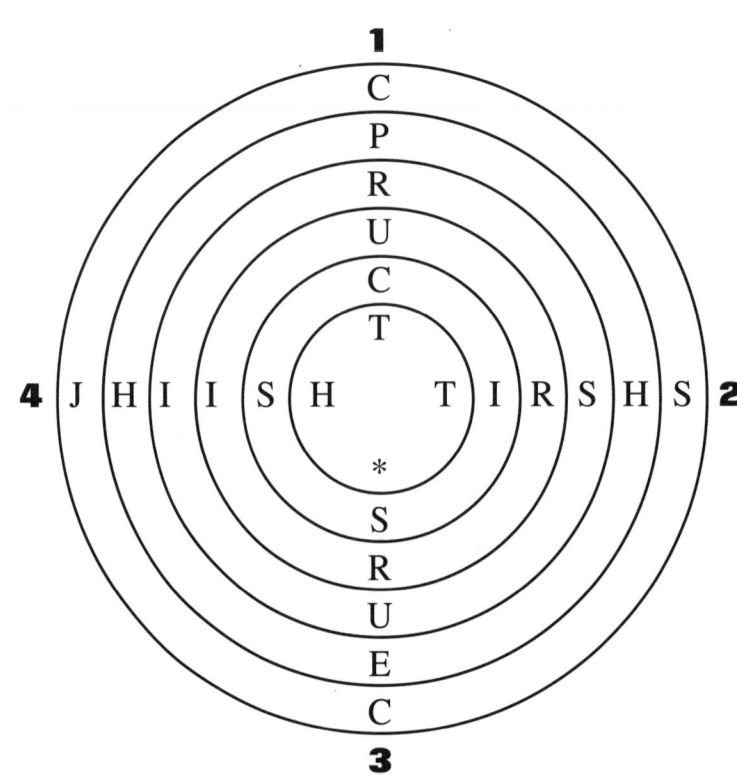

Message

1 _ _ _ _ _ _ _

2 _ _ _ _ _ _ _

3 _ _ _ _ _ _ _

4 _ _ _ _ _ _ _

44   Grades 5 & 6. ©1996 Broadman & Holman, When the Well Runs (Totally and Completely) Dry: Ideas and Activities for Grades 1-6

A Coat of Arms for Stephen (and You!)

In the book of Acts we meet a man of God by the name of Stephen. A "coat of arms" was a shield that told something about a person's life. follow the instructions and design a coat of arms for Stephen. Then design one for yourself.

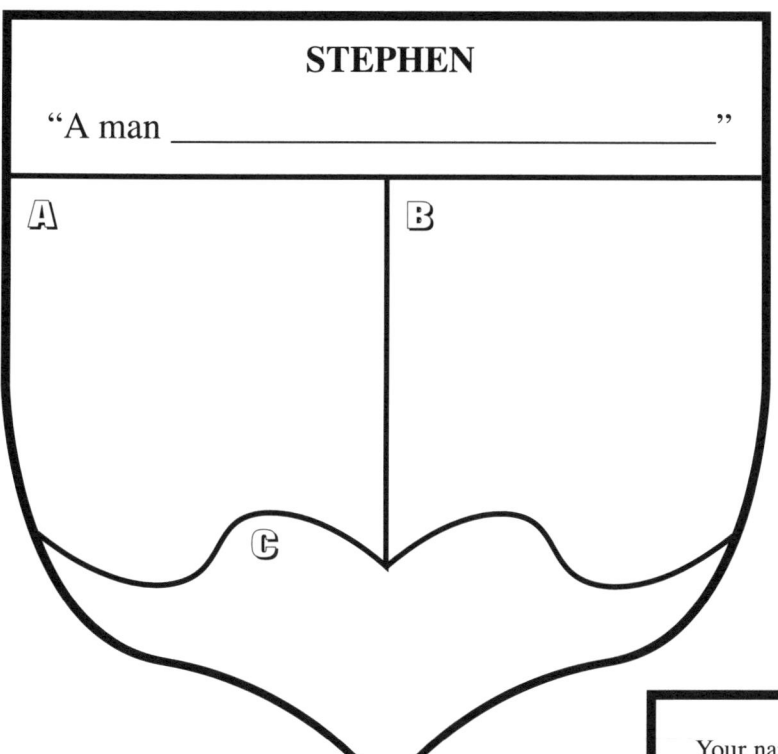

STEPHEN

"A man _____"

A   B

C

See Acts 6:5. How does the writer describe Stephen?

A   Use 3 words and a simple sketch to describe how Stephen helped others (Acts 6:1-5, 8)

B   Use 3 words and a sketch to describe Stephen's death (Acts 7:54-60)

C   Draw a symbol (animal or object) that seems to describe Stephen's life and personality to you.

Your name _____

"A _____ full of _____ and _____."

D   E

F

D   Use 3 words and a sketch to describe something good you have done for others.

E   Use 3 words and a sketch to describe what kind of person you want to be when you grow up.

F   Draw a symbol that would describe your personality.

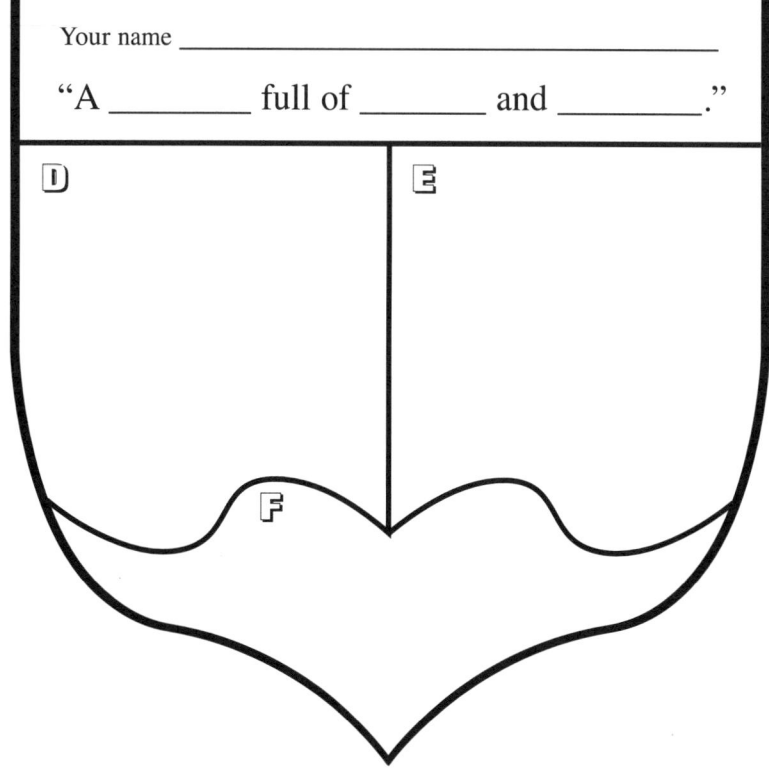

Grades 5 & 6. ©1996 Broadman & Holman, When the Well Runs (Totally and Completely) Dry: Ideas and Activities for Grades 1-6

The Bible Adds Up!

Have you ever noticed how interesting numbers can be? Numbers are also important in the Bible. Remember how Jonah stayed in the belly of the fish for 3 nights and 3 days? That number turned out to be a clue for how long Jesus would stay in the tomb. (See Matthew 12:40) When you read the Bible, watch for numbers and ask yourself, "Hmmmm...I wonder if that number means something special?" Find out by asking your parents or teacher or pastor. Or ask them to show you how to look up number words in a Bible Concordance—-and become a Bible detective!

Place the numbers in the circles so that the sum of the numbers is the same in each direction. Then match the sum to the corresponding verse. (Hint: Two of the number puzzles have the same answer.)

Example:

Use numbers 1, 2, 3, 4, & 5

Sum: __9__

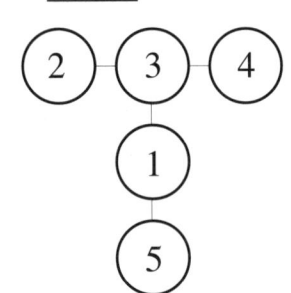

Use numbers 1, 2, 3, 4, 5, 6, & 7

Sum:_____

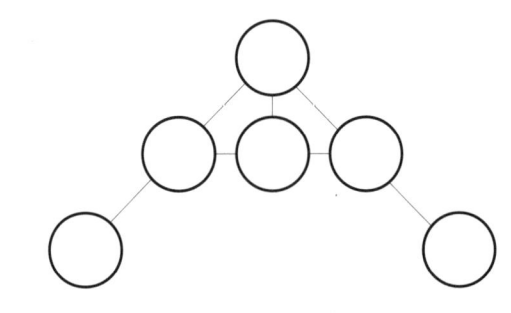

Use numbers 1, 2, 3, 4, 5, 6, & 7

Sum:_____

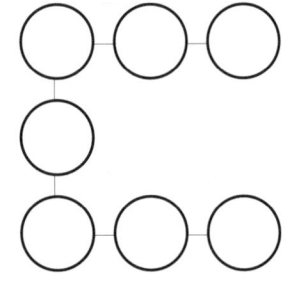

Use numbers 1, 2, 3, 4, 5, 6, 7, & 8

Sum:_____

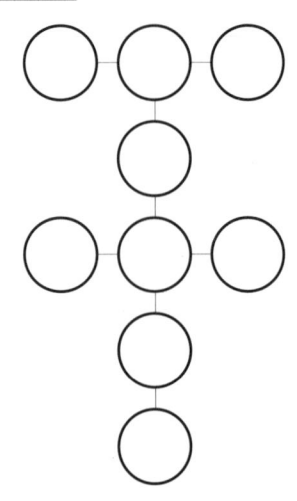

Ⓐ Galatians 1:18 Paul stayed with Peter _____ days

Ⓑ Luke 17:17 Jesus healed 10 lepers. How many did not come back to thank Him?_____

Ⓒ Mark 16:14 Jesus appeared to the _____ disciples. (Be sure to look this one up!)